# MODERN SPY STORIES

TIME: DATE: ALTITUDE: 1,297m FLIGHT SPEED: 1400km/h

TARGET 1 TARGET 3
TARGET 2 TARGET 4

BY EMMA HUDDLESTON

MOMENTUM

Published by The Child's World®
1980 Lookout Drive • Mankato, MN 56003-1705
800-599-READ • www.childsworld.com

Photographs ©: Billion Photos/Shutterstock
Images, cover (soldier), 1 (soldier); Wind Vector/
Shutterstock Images, cover (computer screen), 1
(computer screen); Red Line Editorial, 5; Soeren
Stache/picture-alliance/dpa/AP Images, 6;
iStockphoto, 9; Everett Historical/Shutterstock
Images, 10; Everett Collection/Newscom, 11;
Rena Schild/Shutterstock Images, 12; Daniel J.
Macy/Shutterstock Images, 14; Kathy deWitt/
Alamy, 16; J'rg Carstensen/picture-alliance/dpa/
AP Images, 17; John Minchillo/AP Images, 18; Matt
Sullivan/Reuters/Newscom, 20; Tom Uhlman/AP
Images, 23; Starikov Pavel/Shutterstock Images,
24; Pavel Ptitsin/AP Images, 27; Ivan Vodop'janov/
Kommersant/Sipa USA/AP Images, 28

ISBN 9781503844841 (Reinforced Library Binding)
ISBN 9781503847286 (Portable Document Format)
ISBN 9781503848474 (Online Multi-user eBook)
LCCN 2019956598

Printed in the United States of America

# CONTENTS

MOMENTUM

# FAST FACTS

### Modern Wars

▶ Many wars have happened since 1990. Outside nations sometimes get involved. They support one side over another. For example, the United States supported Kuwait during the Persian Gulf War (1990–1991). It sent troops and supplies.

### Spies and Their Tools Today

▶ The public doesn't know a lot about modern spies. Many spies are still working. Their identity may be a secret. With the help of spies, a country can protect its land and people from danger.

▶ Some countries spy to stay updated on another country's activities. The United States and Russia have been known to spy on each other.

▶ Some countries spy on others to get advanced technology.

▶ Technology is a major part of spying today. Spies often use computers, satellites, and drones to get information. Drones are flying devices with cameras.

▶ Computer **hackers** steal information online. They can break into stored **data** or take over a computer's control system.

# Modern Conflicts

There have been many conflicts since the 1990s, and only some are listed below. In many types of conflicts, spies are needed to get information about an enemy.

**1990–1991** — **Persian Gulf War**
Fought in the Middle East between Iraq and Kuwait, with countries such as the United States supporting Kuwait.

**1990–1994** — **Rwanda Civil War**
Fought between two groups of people in East Africa's Rwanda. Horrible mass murders occurred during this conflict.

**1991–2002** — **Sierra Leone Civil War**
Rebels from Liberia and Sierra Leone in West Africa teamed up to fight the Sierra Leone army.

**2003–2011** — **Iraq War**
U.S. and British forces invaded Iraq to defeat leader Saddam Hussein. Then, U.S. forces had to fight other rebel groups.

**2001–2014 (formal combat mission ended)** — **Afghanistan War**
The United States went to Afghanistan to defeat a group that had attacked the United States.

**2011–ongoing in 2020** — **Syrian Civil War**
Fought between the Syrian government and its people who wanted a different way of life. Many other countries, including the United States, have gotten involved in this conflict.

# CHAPTER ONE

# SPY IN THE GULF WAR

In 1990, Albert Sombolay walked down a street in Berlin, Germany. He looked over his shoulder. Then, he crossed the street and walked into the **embassy** for the country of Jordan. He was a soldier in the U.S. Army. But he wasn't on a mission for his country. Sombolay was planning to spy against the United States by trading information for money.

It was December, and the Persian Gulf War was heating up. Iraq had invaded Kuwait four months earlier. Countries such as Egypt and the United States rushed to help Kuwait. They sent troops to nearby Saudi Arabia. They hoped the soldiers would stop Iraq from attacking. Iraq wanted control of oil in Kuwait and Saudi Arabia. Jordan supported Iraq.

At the embassy, Sombolay saw snow falling outside the window. He sat down to speak with a Jordanian official.

◄ **Jordan has dozens of embassies all over the world. One is in Germany.**

Sombolay gave up valuable information about the U.S. military. He talked about U.S. troops being sent to Saudi Arabia. In fact, Sombolay's troop was going to Saudi Arabia soon. He offered to take photos of his team and their activities there. The Jordanian officials were interested in getting the inside scoop about part of the U.S. Army. They took his information. They gave him $1,300 in return for spying.

For months, Iraqi troops stayed in Kuwait. The United States and its supporters realized Iraq might not leave without a fight. They formed a plan called Operation Desert Storm. It was an air attack on Iraq. It was scheduled for January. When Sombolay went to the Jordan embassy to spy, Operation Desert Storm was only a few weeks away. Sombolay didn't know about the plan.

## STUDENT AND SPY

Ji Chaoqun was a Chinese student studying in the United States in 2015. He sent an email titled "Midterm test questions" to someone in China. But the email wasn't about school. It had background information about eight people China could **recruit** to be spies. Ji used his identity as a student to cover up sending information to China. He wasn't caught until 2018.

▲ **Kuwait is a small country located southeast of Iraq and next to Saudi Arabia.**

But if he helped the enemy find out, Iraq would have time to prepare a defense.

Before leaving for Saudi Arabia, Sombolay made plans to meet with an undercover agent from Jordan. But he was caught while going to the meeting. He was arrested by U.S. officials. He spent 12 years in jail before being released in 2003.

▲ **Many army vehicles were destroyed in the conflict.**

Since Sombolay was caught so quickly, his spying did not have major effects on Operation Desert Storm. However, if he had successfully sent secret photos to the enemy, he could have stopped the operation from working as planned.

**Iraqi forces were eventually defeated ▶ in part because of air strikes.**

# CHAPTER TWO

# COMPUTER HACKER

E dward Snowden walked down a tiled hallway at work in the early 2010s. He pushed a cart with an old computer on it. The computer hadn't been used by anyone for a while. At least, that's what other people thought. Snowden had been secretly storing lots of files on it.

Suddenly, Snowden was stopped in the hallway. A man wanted to know what he was doing with the old computer. Snowden paused. He hadn't prepared a fake story to cover up his actions. So he said, "Stealing secrets." Both men looked at each other and laughed. The worker thought Snowden was joking and walked away. Snowden pushed the cart on and breathed a sigh of relief. His spy work was still a secret.

Snowden worked for the U.S. Central Intelligence Agency (CIA) and National Security Agency (NSA) from 2006 to 2013.

◄ Some people supported Edward Snowden's spy work.

▲ **The CIA headquarters is in Langley, Virginia.**

He helped the NSA with cybersecurity projects. In other words, he helped protect important online data from being stolen by hackers. The reason Snowden was good at cybersecurity was because he was a skilled computer hacker himself.

Snowden learned about Chinese **surveillance** systems while working for the CIA. He found out that China was watching its own citizens. Snowden wondered if the United States was, too. So he looked deeper into U.S. surveillance systems.

Snowden was worried about what he found. In 2013, he flew to Hong Kong. Snowden walked through a busy airport. He had decided to share what he found with the world. Snowden met with journalists in Hong Kong. He gave them computer files full of secret documents that he had discovered while spying. What he found seemed to prove that the United States was spying on its own citizens. He found out the NSA stored the phone records of millions of people. It was also watching what people did on the internet.

## SPY SATELLITES

Satellites in space use cameras to take pictures and videos. They pick up detailed shots. They send data back to Earth while in space. Satellites from the U.S. Department of Defense are used for many reasons. The military watches troop movements with them. The government also uses them to watch out for natural disasters. Some people worry the government uses satellites to spy on people.

**International**

**Secret back door enables NSA to spy on messages of US citizens**

New Snowden revelation
on emails and phone calls

Law-abiding Americans
'spied on without warrant'

James Ball and Spencer Ackerman

The National Security Agency has a secret back door into its databases under a legal authority enabling it to search for US citizens' email and phone calls without a warrant, according to a top secret document passed to the Guardian by Edward Snowden.

The previously undisclosed rule change allows NSA operatives to hunt for individual Americans' communications using their name or other identifying information, senator Ron Wyden told the Guardian.

The authority enables "warrantless searches for the phone calls or emails of law-abiding Americans".

The authority, approved in 2011, is in contrast with repeated assurances by Barack Obama and senior intelligence officials to both Congress and the public that the privacy of US communications is protected from the NSA's dragnet programs.

The data is being gathered under section 702 of the of the Fisa

You can
that har
$77m-a
Winfre

Adam Gabba

The Swiss tou
Oprah Winfr
tered racisr
Zurich told
to look at w
The me
richest w
on US te
had refu
$38,000
The
an inte
about
Butle
Ame
his
ev

▲ **Newspapers around the world published Snowden's story.**

The journalists were shocked. They wrote reports about what Snowden found. Then, they published them. Within a few days, the United States accused Snowden of spying. It ordered people in Hong Kong to arrest him. But Snowden fled. He went to Moscow, Russia, where he could live without fear of being sent back to the United States.

Some people in the United States believe Snowden betrayed his country by spying and leaking information. But Snowden is glad he shared what he found. He thinks people should know if their government is watching them.

**Snowden sometimes speaks to crowds over ▶ web conferences. He can't travel to Western countries because they might send him back to the United States.**

# CHAPTER THREE

# SPYING FOR NEW TECHNOLOGY

**B**en Glassman stood behind a wooden stand. It held many microphones that pointed toward him. Glassman laid his hands on the wooden top. A room full of people looked at him. Glassman was a U.S. attorney. As he took a breath and spoke, cameras in the room started recording.

Glassman announced that Chinese spy Yanjun Xu would face **espionage** charges in court. This was the first time a spy had been captured and brought to the United States for trial.

Xu began spying for China in 2013. He targeted **aviation** companies around the world. In 2017, Xu messaged an engineer at GE Aviation, a U.S. company. It made jet engines and fan blades. Xu focused on getting design details for new products.

◀ **U.S. attorney for the Southern District of Ohio Ben Glassman spoke to reporters about Yanjun Xu.**

▲ **GE Aviation employees work hard on designing and building GE products.**

If Xu got the information for China, it would be bad for the United States. U.S. businesses making the aircraft and technology would have to compete with Chinese businesses that copied their work. Also, the U.S. military wouldn't benefit as much from advanced technology. That's because the Chinese military would know what was being made and could copy it.

Xu invited the engineer from GE Aviation to China. He pretended to work for a science and technology group. He offered the engineer $3,500. He also said the engineer could speak at a well-known Chinese university. The engineer agreed. Xu asked the engineer to create a folder of a few files for his speech. Xu's goal was to get secrets about how new U.S. aircraft were made.

## SPYING WITH DRONES

The U.S. military flies drones to spy on enemy troops and areas overseas, but some drones also fly over U.S. land. In 2017, the U.S. government stopped flying hundreds of drones. It was worried that China was stealing information that the drones gathered. That's because the drones were made in China or with Chinese parts.

These drones were mainly used to inspect U.S. land and natural disasters. For example, they helped emergency workers take care of wildfires and floods. But since the information showed details of U.S. land, it could be used by an enemy to plan an attack. The United States decided that not flying the drones was the safest option. They wanted to investigate whether China could take the information from them.

The engineer flew to China. He met Xu for lunch the day he gave his presentation. Before speaking, a Chinese official put a memory stick into the engineer's computer. His computer had secret GE company files on it, and China was hoping to get them.

The U.S. government suspected something. The engineer was questioned when he came back home. The Federal Bureau of Investigation (FBI) wanted to catch Xu. It worked with the engineer. Together, they sent Xu more files from GE Aviation to trick him. Then, Xu and the engineer arranged to meet in Belgium. Xu didn't realize he was being sent into a trap.

Xu traveled to Belgium. It was Sunday. He walked through the airport and sat down to wait for the engineer, but the man never came. Instead, a group of police officers and FBI agents approached Xu. His mission was stopped. He was arrested and brought to the United States for trial.

**GE Aviation has worked with the U.S. government ▶ to build engines for military planes.**

# CHAPTER FOUR

# SOCIAL SPY

**M**aria Butina looked around at the restaurant where she was hosting her birthday party. People were laughing and talking to each other. Every time someone opened the restaurant door, a crisp autumn breeze cooled down the people nearby. It was November 12, 2016. Butina walked through the room, greeting her guests. Some guests were just friends. Others worked in politics. Butina had lots of social connections. Her relationships with officials in Russia and the United States helped her gather information as a spy for Russia.

No one knows exactly what her spy work was. But Butina said she wanted to make the relationship between the United States and Russia friendly. So, she was interested in information about politics. She supported leaders who were open to partnering with Russia.

◄ **Maria Butina wanted to help sway U.S. politics so it favored Russia.**

Butina was a Russian **national**. She moved to Washington, DC, in 2016 to attend American University. She was known for supporting gun rights. In other words, she believed people should be able to own guns. For a few years before coming to the United States, Butina worked in Moscow. She was an assistant at a bank. Her boss was Alexander Torshin. He was also a big supporter of gun rights.

Butina traveled to the United States many times in the 2010s. Sometimes, she and Torshin traveled together. They went to National Rifle Association (NRA) meetings. The NRA supports gun rights in the United States. They met many top NRA officials. Butina wanted to get to know U.S. officials better. That way, she would have more chances to **influence** them. She could encourage U.S. leaders to be friendly with Russia.

One of the U.S. officials Butina met was Paul Erickson. He worked for Republican political leaders. He also worked with groups such as the NRA. One time, Erickson helped the NRA raise money at an event. Through his work, Erickson made connections to many political leaders. From 2013 to 2015, Butina got closer to Erickson. Meanwhile, she also got closer to U.S. political leaders.

In 2015, Butina sat at her desk. She typed an email to Erickson. It was about a project called "Diplomacy."

▲ Butina and Alexander Torshin worked together. Torshin was a Russian politician and banker.

Butina revealed her goal to influence U.S. politics. She knew the 2016 U.S. presidential election was coming up. She wanted to make sure the next president would be friendly with Russia.

A few months before the election, Erickson emailed one of Donald Trump's workers. Trump was running for president.

▲ Butina got a warm welcome
when she returned to Russia.

Erickson tried to set up a meeting between Trump and Russian
president Vladimir Putin. In some people's opinion, these emails
were evidence of Butina's plan working.

After Trump was elected, some U.S. officials thought that
Butina's friendships with Torshin and Erickson seemed suspicious.

Butina was a link that connected Russian officials to Republican leaders in the United States. After Trump won, Butina bragged that she helped him communicate with Russia during his **campaign**. This information caused people to stop and think. They wondered whether Republicans got help or money from Russia to win the presidency. The FBI investigated Butina. It looked at her messages with Torshin and Erickson. Butina was arrested in 2018 for working as a Russian agent. In 2019, she was sent back to Moscow.

## THINK ABOUT IT

► People can spy for their job. Some work for the government or military. What types of spying do you think are most dangerous and important? What types are the most interesting? Explain you answers.

► Why do you think countries want to spy on the United States, even though they aren't at war with the United States?

► How do you think spies today are different from spies in the 1800s or 1900s?

# GLOSSARY

**aviation (ay-vee-AY-shun):** Aviation means being related to aircrafts. Some people from China want to steal U.S. aviation secrets.

**campaign (kam-PAYN):** A campaign is a series of organized events to help someone become well-known and well-liked by voters. Trump's presidential campaign was a success.

**data (DAY-tuh):** Data is facts, numbers, and information stored in computers. Spies can use data to learn about another country.

**embassy (EM-buh-see):** An embassy is a building in one country with offices for leaders of another country. Sombolay went to the Jordan embassy to sell U.S. secrets.

**espionage (ES-pee-uh-nahzh):** Espionage is the act of spying, especially on another company or government. Xu was charged with espionage.

**hackers (HAK-urz):** Hackers are people who use computer codes to break into another computer or online storage base. Hackers can steal important government information.

**influence (IN-floo-uhns):** Influence means to change the results of an action or the way a decision is made. Butina wanted to influence U.S. politics to help Russia.

**national (NASH-uh-nuhl):** A national is a person who supports or works for a certain country no matter where he or she lives. The spy was a Russian national living in the United States.

**recruit (ri-KROOT):** To recruit means to try to get someone to join something. China tried to recruit spies.

**surveillance (ser-VAY-luhns):** Surveillance systems have the ability to watch someone or something closely. Snowden checked out U.S. surveillance systems.

# TO LEARN MORE

## BOOKS

Briggs, Andy. *How to Be an International Spy.*
New York, NY: Lonely Planet Kids, 2015.

Ringstad, Arnold. *What's Inside a Drone?*
Mankato, MN: The Child's World, 2020.

Spradlin, Michael P. *Ryan Pitts: Afghanistan: A Firefight in the Mountains of Wanat.* New York, NY: Farrar Straus Giroux, 2019.

## WEBSITES

Visit our website for links about modern spies: **childsworld.com/links**

*Note to Parents, Teachers, and Librarians: We routinely verify our Web links to make sure they are safe and active sites. So encourage your readers to check them out!*

## SELECTED BIBLIOGRAPHY

Healy, Melissa. "GI Imprisoned for Espionage in Gulf War."
*Los Angeles Times*, 4 Dec. 1991, latimes.com. Accessed 26 Nov. 2019.

MacAskill, Ewen. "Snowden." *Guardian*, 13 Sept. 2019, theguardian.com. Accessed 26 Nov. 2019.

"Maria Butina: Russian Agent Deported from US to Moscow."
*BBC News*, 26 Oct. 2019, bbc.com. Accessed 26 Nov. 2019.

# INDEX

## ABOUT THE AUTHOR

Emma Huddleston lives in Minnesota with her husband. She enjoys writing children's books and thinks spies are a fascinating part of history!